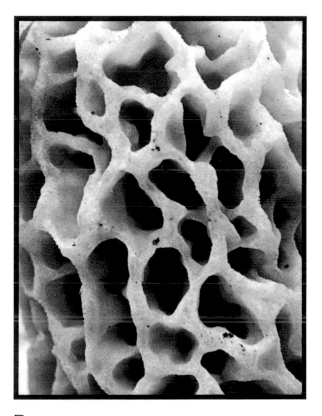

ROON (roon) n. 1. A person possessed by extreme or insatiable desires for morel mushrooms. 2. A keeper of the secrets and Order of Roon. 3. One who is given to luxury and sensual pleasures. 4. Used in cooking, an equivalent measurement of dried, frozen or fresh morel mushrooms.

THE MOREL
MUSHROOM
INFORMATION / RECIPES / LORE

THE MOREL MUSHROOM

INFORMATION / RECIPES / LORE

A GUIDE FOR ROONS

BY JOHN RATZLOFF
RECIPES BY JERRY PETERMEIER

Voyageur Press

Dedicated in loving memory to Paul Chelgren who, moments before his death, bequeathed his favorite fishing hole to his brother but refused to tell him where it was.

Copyright © 1990 by John Ratzloff

Printed in Hong Kong
90 91 92 93 94 5 4 3 2 1

This is a revised and expanded edition of *Roon: A Tribute to Morel Mushrooms* by John Ratzloff published by Cabin Publishing, Long Lake, Minnesota.

ISBN 0-89658-128-4

Library of Congress Cataloging-in-Publication Data available upon request.

This edition published by
Voyageur Press, Inc.
P.O. Box 338
123 North Second Street
Stillwater, MN 55082 U.S.A.
In Minn 612-430-2210
Toll-free 800-888-9653

Voyageur Press books are also available at discounts for quantities for educational, fundraising, premium, or sales-promotion use. For details contact the marketing manager. Please write or call for our free catalog of publications.

Roon (roon) n. 1. A person possessed by extreme or insatiable desires for morel mushrooms. 2. A keeper of the secrets and Order of Roon. 3. One who is given to luxury and sensual pleasures. 4. Used in cooking, an equivalent measurement of dried, frozen or fresh morel mushrooms.

CONTENTS

INTRODUCTION

This book goes far beyond a mere tribute. It has taken the morel to a height of celebration, a celebration to be shared and enjoyed by all the senses.

All too often books dealing with matters mycological can be stuffy, filled with facts and obscure information, providing the reader with little enthusiasm. Not so with *The Morel Mushroom*. This book is an adventure story.

The Morel Mushroom takes a more lighthearted view of this regal fungus. From the thrill of the hunt through the delight of the feast, *The Morel Mushroom* explores the realm of the morel in a manner to be enjoyed now and to be remembered for seasons to come.

It is truly a welcome and refreshing approach to morels.

—Lee M. Muggli, Minnesota Mycological Society; Vice-President, North American Mycological Association.

FOREWORD

I have occasioned upon the inspirational sort, the kind of person likely to finish a declaration with "praise the Lord" or utter a speech with rigorous inflection rising to the brink of exaltation. I've also met others who behave less drastically when enlivened by a sweeping sensation, perhaps resulting in a Saturday afternoon of yardwork, or possibly even an enthusiastic attempt at a jog around the neighborhood. Regardless of the source, it may be admitted that a person inspired is a person at his foolish best. With that thought in mind I am compelled to inquire: Have you ever met anyone inspired by a mushroom?

John Ratzloff is such a person and with the skill of Jerry Petermeier he has seen fit to devote his considerable creative talents to the spectrum of the morel mushroom.

For most, the delight of the morel, or any mushroom, might be realized in an ambitious omelet or expensive entrée. But in the customs of John and Jerry this delight is elevated to a ritual of sight, touch, sound and taste—in that order. Like all wild game, the morel is elusive prey and to acquire a full larder of these delicacies the search must be approached as a craft. A refined roon, such as John or Jerry, masters this craft with keen senses, know-how and the ability to relax. Their methods are not easy to teach but they are easy to learn. A student of the Order of Roon simply cannot be led promptly to the quarry. Rather, he can be directed to the woods, his eyes trained to the ground and instructed to carefully explore the world at his feet.

Clearly there is more to the morel than a simple sensory delight, although, when pulled from a supermarket shelf, a morel can provide only that. Yet, like crappies snared by your own hook or pie made from backyard apples, the morel acquires new dimensions of taste when preceded by a day of prospecting. Furthermore, after obtaining these sponge-like dainties, it would be the height of folly to lack the means or knowledge to prepare them; hence this book.

From Jerry Petermeier comes knowledge. A rustic and hospitable figure, Jerry has tread more miles and lived more hours in the woods than some animals. Consequently, he lives by a credo of utility. He borrows his wares from the woods and has shaped his ethos from the doctrines of nature. Nevertheless, Jerry is by no means a pure man. He has at least one indulgence that, in effect, becomes a benefit to everyone else—namely, food. Imagine a man living in an isolated cabin far removed from overstocked supermarket shelves and holding a strong aversion to stew from a tin. Imagine a tireless explorer probing and sorting, testing the goods grown in his expansive backyard until he satisfies his fancy for the finest in taste. This is Jerry's skill, and the products of his skill are original. His dishes are the simple formulation of what has been tried and proved wildly successful.*

Add to this one rousing pour of John Ratzloff. Ever since the day he kicked the successful life in the shins and bolted with nothing but a wooden duck, he has been on a binge of inquiry. After having discovered the turbulent desires of expression, which had been squeezed

---

* Jerry measures how good his recipes are by the volume of food he gets on the ceiling during preparation.

off by the Monday-thru-Friday, golf-on-Saturday existence, John began to experiment fervently. Through the lens of a camera he started to re-explore both his own talent and the world around him, educating his eyes in the art of framing, focusing and judging the nuances of sunlight. Consequently his photographs evoke a strong sense of the aesthetic, but the colors and textures mean nothing to John without acuity and fidelity. Nowhere is this more evident than in this book.

Most certainly John's work extends beyond the visual. In his former wing-tip world he was considered an "idea man," someone who could envision a viable concept and expand it to realization. But John's ideas were irresistibly laced with an irreverence that did not root well in the corporate environment. The alternative for John was to paddle his own canoe knowing that he would rather do his own task imperfectly than another's well. With the morel mushroom he defined this task and also discovered something too good to be denied, especially by people who abhor fad and imitation and are not terribly fond of plastic. For these people—potential roons—John Ratzloff and Jerry Petermeier offer this book, an inspired work.

—Peter Wahlstrom

John Ratzloff

ROON

A morel is a mushroom. A mushroom is a toadstool. A mushroom or toadstool is a fungus. More than one fungus is fungi or funguses. Fungi are a large group of plants without chlorophyl, including yeasts, molds, mushrooms and smuts. Wood nymphs usually hang out around mushrooms. Avoid wood nymphs loitering near a smut.

Morel mushrooms have been driving people over the edge of moderation for centuries. During the Middle Ages the people of what are now Poland, Germany and Czechoslovakia merrily burned forests to the ground after determining that ashes serve as prime morel fertilizer. They simply wanted to ensure a more bountiful harvest.

Fortunately, such extremes have not been pursued to harvest common button mushrooms, which are packed in cans or plastic and sold in food markets. The difference between morels and button mushrooms, however, is like the difference between cheese and chalk. The great Herb Harper, roon of roons, once remarked, "Compared to morels, button mushrooms have the flavor of fairly good cardboard." (Button mush-

room jokes are common roon procedure, or CRP.) In fact, the filet mignon flavor and texture of the morel are notable for their combined exquisiteness. Yet it is a proper supplement to a main dish, adding dimension without overpowering richness. Enhancing this flavor is an aroma that can best be appreciated while the morel is sautéed with bubbling butter in a skillet. The nose treat is a sensuous one, earthy lust in full bloom.

Besides engendering a three-ring circus of the senses, morels also nourish the spirit. Their brief emergence coincides with the season of rebirth and beauty, when Nature springs awake with a sweeping mandate for all her subjects to breed. Seeking morels during this time puts lead in your pencil. The spirit cannot claim immunity from the edicts of Nature, and the senses cannot resist interaction with the morel itself, from the first sighting to the eventual tasting. Morels work in conjunction with Nature, providing incentive for seekers to return enthusiastically every spring and, thus, bring out people's unexpected, refreshing extremes otherwise known as common roon behavior (CRB).

THE MEDIUM IS THE MUSHROOM

Morels grow in temperate zones throughout the world. They have been found as far north as the Soviet Union and as far south as Australia. In the People's Republic of China, they are known as "sheep stomachs" and are used to treat stomach disorders as well as being enjoyed for their taste. Romania and England celebrate the morel with colorful, decorative watercolor paintings on fine china cups. Curiously, morels plucked in Pakistan and France are exported and sold from Michigan to Manhattan even though they are well-known and omnipresent in the United States. In Minnesota the morel is recognized as the official state fungus.

The extensive habitat of the morel is certainly a factor in its expanding universal appeal and this prominence may properly be considered the medium. The message of the medium, therefore, is the message of the morel. What could possibly be the message of a mushroom? Suppose, for a minute, that the negotiators at the famous "walk in the woods" disarmament conference had opened their minds to the undeniable logic of those woods and their eyes to the world at their feet. Suppose a herd of morels had caught their glance and immediately the somber tension dictating the dialogue lifted as each raved about the marvelous flavor and laughed about recent morel outings back in the home country. Suppose they stopped to pluck, sharing recipes and opinions, a first opportunity provided by one tiny cultural link to find a beginning and build an understanding through which politics and protocol might be transcended. Fear of that ghastly, man-made mushroom supplanted by mutual positive feelings for the most cherished and benign mushroom Nature has to offer.

FINDING AND EATING MORELS

Morel mushrooms contain large amounts of vitamin D (required for normal bone growth) and have almost no calories, though, when cooking, they will absorb amazing quantities of butter. Their appearance and texture are distinctive, like that of a small sea sponge and are so unmistakable that experts agree a spore print for positive identification is unnecessary. Moreover, in the wide variety of mushrooms, where at least some level of toxicity is always present and error can result in much more than an upset stomach, morels possess the characteristic of being very safe to eat. There are only these few precautions to eating morels:

1) Do not eat raw morels.

2) Do not eat morels that show signs of decay—just as you would not eat a rotten peach.

3) Just as a few unfortunate people are allergic to strawberries, tomatoes or potatoes, similar reactions may occur with morels. Consequently, when eating morels for the first time, small amounts are recommended to test for allergic reaction.

4) It is likely that morels were a featured item on the menu at the notorious banquets of the Caesars. There is an overwhelming urge to consume conspicuous quantities of morels. Overindulgence got to Julius Caesar…it can get to you.

5) There is a false morel called *Gyromitra* that is controversial. *Gyromitra* is a species of mushroom that is edible and delicious in many areas of the United States while it is dangerously toxic in other areas. The *Gyromitra's* cap looks like a brain, with convolutions and folds rather than the distinctive pits and ridges of the morel. If you are unsure about a *Gyromitra,* do not eat one…don't even think about it.*

Morels consist of a cap and stem, hollow throughout, that are joined together in one continuous piece. They are the only spring mushrooms with pitted and ridged caps and, conveniently, there are no dangerous mushrooms resembling morels that appear at the same time of year. Thus, beginners (would-be roons) may seek, pluck and eat morels with confidence.

Morels grow from the earth giving the appearance of a pinecone-strewn ground with a "Salvador Dali" difference: All of the morels stand erect, a sight that makes knees tremble, hearts pound and lips shake with a slight but rapid involuntary motion.

In the United States, itinerant roons begin plucking morels during January in southern California, during March in the south and southwest, eventually following the spring warming and its accompanying rains to the northern temperate zones in May. When and where there is spring, there are likely to be morels, and roons. Prime morel plucking seasons last only about two weeks. An individual specimen will emerge and wither in four to six days.

Morels are distributed nearly as widely as cigarettes. They grow from the sides of mountains, on forest floors, in pasture land, in backyards of homes, in ditches along railroad tracks,

*"There are old mushroom eaters and there are bold mushroom eaters. There are no old bold mushroom eaters." *Joy of Cooking.*

even between the cracks of your neighbor's sidewalk. In addition they are inclined to re-appear each spring in the same location, as do roons. Just as there is never only one mouse in a house, there is no such thing as only one morel in the woods. They are normally found in groups, known as herds, with the exception of a lone morel that may stand displaced from the herd, like a solo oboist. Such a morel is called a scout, and, if it can be located, a herd is usually hiding within a fifty-foot radius.

Fungi are plants that chemically digest organic matter, absorbing nutrients and recycling wastes to build transformed cell structure. Without fungal feeding the forests of the world would eventually smother themselves in their own debris. Morels, simply put, are the custodi-ans and disposal plants of nature—the fruit of ashes to ashes and dust to dust—and knowing their preferred food supplies is the logical place to begin searching for them. Journeyman roons offer this list of known morel food sources and ideal growing habitats:

They are found in:
    uncompacted soil
    ashes of last year's forest fires
    rich garden soil
    sandy soil
    clay soil

They are found near:
    stands of aspen and birch
    young second growths of hardwood
    recently dead or dying elms
    spruce stumps
    the edges of conifer forests
    walnut and butternut trees
    old apple, cherry and peach orchards

They are found on:
    banks of rivers, swamps and streams
    pasture lands near water

Or they are found along:
    natural drainages of ravines
    game trails
    rural railroad tracks

And they are found wherever:
    bracken fern grows

Morels belong to the genus *Morchella,* which is Latin for "mushroom"—roons secretly refer to them as "Helens," as in Helen of Troy. Over sixty species have been identified with five of the most common and desirable ones de-scribed on the following pages.

ANGUSTICEPS

Morchella angusticeps means "narrow head mushroom" and is also known as the "black" or "slender-cap" morel. *Angusticeps* grows from two to four inches in height, and is the first species of morel to appear in spring.

The pits in the cap of this species are longer than they are wide, like sets of tiny vertical lips, one above the other in connected rows. The cap itself is dishwater gray to gray-tan (inside the pits) and grows darker in color on the ridges as it matures. The stem is buff-gray with a flaky surface, about as long and wide as the cap, and has uneven and curved wrinkles, like an old roon's forehead. *Angusticeps* emerges when lilacs and white violets are in bloom, when oak leaves are about the size of mouse ears and bracken ferns are curled up like a fiddlehead. This mushroom is often found in sandy or clay soil of thinning, mixed woods, usually on the edges of hickory, birch, maple or conifer forests, and exhibits an intense attraction to ashes.

There also exists a "muscle-beach" version of this species that can grow up to seven inches high and four inches wide across the shoulders. This morel grows especially in the Pacific Northwest and in lesser quantities near the Great Lakes and Eastern seaboard. When young they are black, with a large cone-shaped cap that is rounded at the top.

Roons advise that any *angusticeps* be eaten only when young or showing no signs of decay and without alcohol as upset stomachs have been attributed to the combination. *Angusticeps* caps that have turned completely black from age must not be eaten.

ESCULENTA

Morchella esculenta means "edible mushroom" and is the best-known species of morel. This delicious morel has other names, including "sponge morel," "butter sponge," "Minnesota morel," "yellow morel" and "common morel." It may be called "Bob" if so desired.*

Esculenta grows from two to six inches in height and is half as wide as tall. The cap is shaped like a bulbous pinecone, with gray-brown pits that fade in color as the mushroom ages. The pits are routed into the cap in varied patterns, sizes and shapes, more broad and rounded than in other species of morels. The stem is cream-colored, lighter in color than the cap, and turns sepia with age like an old black and white photo. When young the stem is smooth and covered with a white, powdery coating, but it grows faintly wrinkled with age.

Seek *esculenta* on the ground, close to the base of trees, in old apple, peach or cherry orchards, or near the roots of dead or dying elms. *Esculenta* also frequents swampy areas, at the edges of aspen and birch woods and in the ashen remains of recent forest fires. This species of morel usually emerges after *angusticeps*.

*In an exhausting series of field tests, roons determined that morels don't care what they are called. They will stand there, no matter what names are fashioned, or how poorly they're pronounced.

CRASSIPES

In Latin this species is called *Morchella crassipes* or "thick-footed mushroom." Other names for this enormous species are "gigantic morel," "bigfoot," "hulks," "Paul's Bunyan" and "Moby morel." Some roons believe that *crassipes* is a goliath form of *esculenta* because of a close resemblance in its early growth stages. Thus *crassipes* may appear like an *esculenta* late in the fruiting season but may actually double in size one day later, reaching heights from four to twelve inches.

The cap of *crassipes* is tan or brown and usually cone-shaped. When cut lengthwise and laid flat, the pieces resemble animal pelts. The pits are shallow and long (up to ¾ inch), nearly round, and arranged in irregular patterns. The color at the bottom of the pits is yellow-tan, similar to a good French mustard. The stem is off-white or yellow, and the base is notably enlarged and often wrinkled.

This species is very eagerly sought because it is the largest, and extremely delicious. Just a few of these honkers can fill a roon-bag quickly. They are frequently found in rich garden soil, under oak, beech, maple and ash trees, and near dead or dying elms. Other likely areas are near the edges of woods, along game trails and in grassy meadows and pastures. *Crassipes* emerge like leaping whales in late spring after *Morchella esculenta* has come and gone.

DELICIOSA

Morchella deliciosa, as the Latin implies, is a truly delicious species of *Morchella* and, commonly, the last morel of the season to appear. Also known as the "white ridge morel" or "last morel," *deliciosa* is generally small growing from one and a half to two inches high.

The cap is often curved, like a slightly bent version of a gnome's hat, except the mushroom is blunt at the very top. The pits of the cap are long and narrow outlined by pale white ridges that do not darken with age. The stem is white to yellow, bent and generally short, measuring about the same length as the cap, and about two thirds as wide. As with many old roons, there is a slight enlargement at the base.

Deliciosa should be sought and plucked in moist, grassy areas, especially at the edges of mixed woods of elm, maple and ash. These morels also appear in spring after the emergence of *angusticeps* (narrow heads), *esculenta* (butter sponges), and *crassipes* (bigfoot morels).

CONICA

Morchella conica derives its name from its conical shape. It is a slender, dunce-cap-like variation of *esculenta* and grows from three to five inches tall. Its flavor is outrageous.

The *conica* cap is gray to yellow, with lighter colored ridges, and resembles a miniature witch's hat with a customary crook at the top. The pits in the cap are wide, deep and positioned one above the other. The stem is often longer than the cap, paler in color and slenderer. It is also slightly curved, and usually has a scaly surface. The base is as wrinkled as a baby's butt after a warm bath.

Morchella conica grows in abundance, especially during a rainy January on the southern coast of California. It may also be found during mid-spring in cone-bearing or deciduous woods, as well as in grassy clearings in the south and southwest of the United States.

MOREL SEX

Mushrooms are propagated by single-celled reproductive bodies known as spores. Morel spores are yellow colored and are produced in an oblong pod-like sac called an ascus (asci, plural) that is fabricated in the pits of the cap. Millions of these pods stand on end like missile silos within the pits and along the ridges of the cap. When the time and conditions are favorable the asci erupt, creating a micro-macro spore blizzard sending billions of spores to their eventual destinations aided by wind currents, trickling flows of rainwater or Velcro-legged insects. Forest animals, by eating morels, also contribute to the dissemination process as spores eventually fall from lips of deer and chipmunks' whiskers.

If a spore lands in soil with an ample supply of food and water, it may germinate and give the appearance of becoming pregnant. A bump grows on the spore that eventually grows to become a fine thread of simple cells known as hypha. The hyphal thread spreads through the soil, branching out into more and more threads, forming an underground complex, a mesh-like miniature network known as a mycelium. When the mycelium meets another mycelium they unite and fuse together, becoming one network.

During spring, as moisture from melting snow, rain or heavy dew penetrates the soil, the secondary mycelium will develop numerous cells at various locations on its hyphal threads. These cells, then, begin to generate, forming tiny knobs about the size of a knot tied in four-pound test monofilament fishing line. As the temperature increases, specific growth is engineered to bring the knobs into the proximity of warmth and moisture and the metabolism of the cells rapidly accelerates, doubling for every increase of ten degrees, Fahrenheit. At this stage the tiny knob exerts, cell after cell is reproduced, and a tiny, compact cap and stem take form. Following many days under the earth, the tiny cap and stem begin to enlarge and push their way slowly and steadily to the surface. With a proper combination of temperature, loosely compacted earth, moisture, energy, nutrients and a modicum of serendipity, the head promptly swells, puffing and lengthening until it emerges from the earth. In a few hours, or days at most, it will stand erect: a fleshy phenomenon of function and flavor, with the aroma of raw fungal sex.

ORDER OF ROON

Standard Morel Procedures (SMP).

Caution! Failure to comply with the Order of Roon may result in the immediate loss of all the hair on your body.

I. *Respect the Private Property of Others.* Ask for permission to seek morels on private property. This is not a difficult task and often leads to valuable clues helpful in finding herds of morels. For best results, memorize the following words, so that you may repeat them while looking straight into the eyes of the landowner upon whose property you wish to hunt: "Excuse me, squire, I am a roon. I possess secret wisdom which indicates a strong possibility that erect fungi have recently emerged from your forest, fields and fence lines. I am driven by more than idle desire to pluck and bag as many of the fleshy bits as do not elude me. If you so desire, I will readily share a portion of the toadstools with you; beyond this generosity, I will divulge to you an original recipe for sautéed sponge-fungi with sweet and sour loon. My quest is for the bigfoot. It looks like a sponge growing upon a stick and, even now, may be launching spores over your land."

II. *Respect for Privacy of Wildlife.* While hunting morels do not trample or disturb other living creatures of the wild. By all means, gaze at, sniff, listen to and enjoy how other entities live, but remember: True-red roons have better things to do than violating violets or kicking squirrels in the back.

III. *Respect Your Own Privacy.* Roon etiquette requests that the exact location of a morel find is privileged information. Help would-be roons by sharing knowledge and clues that allow them to find their first morel, but don't take the challenge out of it for them.

IV. *Respect a Fellow Roon's Privacy.* Do not ask roons for the exact location of a morel find. However, it is entirely proper to attempt to read their minds.

V. *Know the Law.* Laws against trespassing exist in every state; knowledge and understanding of these are the people's responsibility. In Minnesota, for example, these laws are printed on the fishing license. Be especially aware in national parks. Many do not allow picking of any vegetation, including mushrooms. All laws, though, are not prohibitive. A good case is the enlightened state of Michigan (land of 10,000 roons), where prime morel-plucking territories are actually designated and open for everyone's benefit. (It is no coincidence that hundreds of roons from all over the world follow the morel to Boyne City, Michigan, each year to participate in the World Morel Plucking Contest and Festival.)

MOREL METHODS

The motto of the North American Mycological Society is "The world of wonder at your feet." Besides sounding catchy, this is a revealing statement. The wonder becomes especially profound while searching for morels because imagination fattens when pacing through the woods with eyes intently probing. It is just this enhanced imagination that promotes larger harvests of morel mushrooms.

While briskly moving about and scanning the ground within fifteen to thirty feet, imagine where spores might be carried by wind or water. Use a sturdy walking stick to stir ashes or poke into tall grass. Cover some territory, be determined, but pause occasionally to survey the surroundings. Locate a dying elm. Glance at your feet; you may be standing right beside a morel.

Common roon procedure for a first morel sighting is to smile broadly, approach carefully and quietly from behind, and then, setting the roon-bag down and raising both hands to the mouth, whisper at the top of the lungs, "Thar she blows and bellars!"

That first morel should be promptly enjoyed simply for the satisfying little noise it makes when plucked.* Often the mycelium and hyphal threads can be seen at the base of the stem. Hold the prize to your nose; notice the lusty scent. Examine it at arm's length; inspect the pits and ridges of the cap. Hold it up allowing sunlight to penetrate its translucent flesh. A brief look around will often reveal the herd, which becomes obvious as your eyes learn to penetrate their ingenious camouflage.

To collect morels, use a woven wood fruit-basket or a sturdy, breathable cloth bag large enough to hold a basketball. Do not put other types of mushrooms in the same receptacle with morels as there is a chance one or more might be highly toxic and contaminate the edibles. Carry several smaller bags if you wish to collect other kinds of mushrooms. Roons recommend comfortable footwear, suitable to the terrain where you will be hunting. A long-sleeved shirt or nylon jacket is good protection, and absolutely necessary deep in prickly ash. Eye protection will also aid in confident movement through deep woods or thick brush.

Finding morels is an experience that does not diminish in surprise or intensity with repetition. With each sighting of a morel comes the sense of a little victory that streams through the body and starts hands quivering in anticipation. Peripheral vision expands markedly along with a budding awareness of your connection to the woods and an appreciation for its innocent essence. Like a farmer wedded to his land, a roon comes to learn that Nature's cycle is without beginning or end, while continuously changing. Yet it is useful only if properly cared for and respected as an endowment, not a commodity to be thoughtlessly exploited. If the forests are allowed to stand, to realize their cycles, just one of the benefits will be an inexhaustible and yearly supply of morel mushrooms.

*Plucking of the first morel is preferred practice, but using a pocket knife to cut the stem as close to the ground as possible allows for easier cleaning and is less disturbing to the mycelium. Cutting the morel from the ground minimizes the potential for dehydration and increases the chances for additional fruitings.

MOREL PREPARATIONS

Freshly picked morels, whether to be cooked fresh or frozen, are fragile and require preparation before they begin to decay.

1. Inspect each mushroom, and gently brush off any dirt, leaves or critters.

2. Split each morel in half lengthwise and remove any bugs that may be inside.

3. If your morels are sandy or dirty, brush off as much as you can and rinse them under running water, the less rinsing, the better.*

4. If you must rinse the morels, drain them thoroughly and gently pat them dry with a towel. They are fun to pat, but resist the urge to spank them.

Now the morels are ready for cooking, freezing or storage (covered with a moist cloth) for up to two or three days in the refrigerator.

To freeze fresh morels, lightly sauté them in butter and freeze them along with the butter and juice in sealed plastic bags.

*Using a clean 1" paintbrush to whisk away sand or dirt before putting your morels in the basket will save cleaning time later on and can eliminate the need for flavor-robbing washing.

DRIED MORELS

Drying fresh morels is a valuable process—it enhances their flavor and reduces toxicity. The following are steps for drying morels:

1. Do not wash morels that are going to be dried.
2. Split the mushroom lengthwise. Morels with caps the size of your little finger or smaller can be dried whole, although the drying time is longer than if split.
3. Now the mushrooms can be dried in any number of easy methods:

   a) A stack of window screens across two saw-horses provides many layers and a large drying area. Cover the screens at night with a piece of plastic, leaving the bottom open and the top propped up with a broom handle, like a tent, in order to keep the plastic off the mushrooms and ensure good air circulation. This drying method takes from about four hours to four days depending on humidity, wind, temperature, size and age of the mushrooms, etc.

   b) Use a large needle and strong line to string the morels through the stem. Hang the string of morels in an open window to dry for about two weeks. This method is effective in drying small, whole morels and the unique aroma will have you howling at the moon.

   c) Commercial food dehydrators also do an excellent job of drying morels.

Morels are approximately ninety percent water, and it is important that they be completely dried before storing. When a morel is dry, it will be as brittle as spun glass, snapping if bent even slightly. Store them in loosely covered glass jars, in a light, but not bright, area of your house. Dried morels will keep indefinitely and are a day-brightener when cooked with a hearty meal during a winter blizzard.

Before cooking, however, dried morels must be reconstituted. Here are some simple reconstitution, or rehydration, steps:

1. Remove the stems from the caps and set aside.
2. Soak the dried morel caps in warm water or warm milk for twenty to thirty minutes. One handful of dried morels expands to about two cups when rehydrated.
3. Swish the soaking morels around from time to time. Sniff the liquid. Sniff your fingers.
4. Pour off and strain the liquid (morel liquor in the roon's vernacular) through two layers of cheesecloth or a coffee filter. Save the liquid for soups, sauces or stews.
5. Place the soaked morels in a colander and rinse under running water until all grit is washed away.
6. Carefully pat the mushrooms dry with paper towels.

The dried morel stems and any small bits of caps can be put in a food processor or blender and pulverized to make morel dust which can be used for cooking. Store morel dust in a leather marble pouch and hide it in a secret place around your house. Occasionally, throughout a long winter, remove the pouch and sift the dust through your fingers as if it were gold. Laugh a slightly wicked laugh and modestly return the dust to the pouch and the pouch to its secret hiding place.

MOREL WARE

The following instructions, notions and twelve recipes are part of an overall morel mushroom-eating experience known as MOREL ORGY. The original recipes are the creation of Jerry Petermeier, roon and wild food wizard. The ingredients are staples in many kitchens, or readily available in local stores. Each of the recipes includes cooking techniques that, when practiced, will produce skills very useful in subsequent cooking adventures.

If you have already hunted and procured morels, the rest is easy. But if you wish to expedite the process, morels can be bought. Dried French morels (morilles) are for sale at Zabar's Market, 2245 Broadway (at 80th Street) in New York City for a mere $5.98 per 7/8 ounce.

In addition to a stove, hibachi grill and bamboo skewers, the recommended equipment includes a ten- to twelve-inch cast-iron skillet, a "number three" Chinese cleaver and a good chopping block. Like the morel, these tools are fun, easy, and cheaper to find than to buy. Try a roon-infested flea market or garage sale, or put the word out for a good cast-iron skillet; no Teflon is allowed.* The Order of Roon requires the use of honest equipment. With proper curing, a cast-iron pan can become a family heirloom and some are even adopted as a family member, albeit a silent one.

A number three Chinese vegetable cleaver made with high-carbon steel is a damn good knife and the price is modest—about five dollars in Oriental markets. An American-made cleaver by Dexter is high-carbon stainless steel and the best cleaver made anywhere under ten dollars. A cleaver is a good choice for those who have a drawerful of seldom-used dull knives. Keep the blade sharp with stone and/or steel and use it often. A cleaver will develop cooking skills faster than almost any other kitchen tool. Its large blade surface is also handy for transferring ingredients from the chopping block to the skillet.

A large, two-foot-by-three-foot chopping block or cutting board proves its value time and time again. Find one, buy one or make one. Keep it clean and smelling sweet with baking soda, or occasionally wipe it with vinegar. Use one side for cutting meat and the other for chopping vegetables. Carve your initials in it.

---

* Research at Michigan State University recently revealed that morels find Teflon™ embarrassing.

ABOUT THESE RECIPES

The recipes for MOREL ORGY use a butter and flour roux for thickening the soups, sauces and gravies. To create this roux, use two tablespoons of flour and two tablespoons of butter with up to two cups of morel liquor. Melt the butter, stir in the flour and cook over medium heat. Add the morel liquor, whisk, return to the heat and whisk again until thick.

To sauté, place the skillet over medium high heat until the butter foams. Add the ingredients to be sautéed in the order called for by the recipe. Whisk them around in the skillet until cooked (about four minutes for a handful of morels). Fresh morels that are wet from rinsing or dried morels wet from rehydrating should be gently dried with a paper towel to remove excess water prior to sautéing.

Two recipes—Morel Dust Soup and Wood Nymph Gravy—require the use of dried morels and the resulting morel liquor. The balance of the recipes can be prepared using either dried and rehydrated, frozen or freshly plucked morels. One roon of morels is equivalent to the approximate volume and weight of the measures below:

1 roon equals 2 cups of frozen morels and butter mixture

1 roon equals 2 cups of halved, medium size fresh morel caps

1 roon equals 1 handful of dried morels, which yields 2 cups of rehydrated morels

2½ pounds of fresh morels equal 1 quart of frozen morels

1 gallon of dried morels weighs from 8 to 10 ounces

10 pounds of fresh morels yield about 1 pound of dried morels

MOREL ORGY

MENU OF RECIPES

1. Shore Lunch
2. Sautéed Morels "Ne Plus Ultra"
3. Morchella Eggsculenta
4. Morels with Bluegill, Red Ear, Pumpkin Seed, and Calico Bream
5. Morels with Steak, Black and Blue
6. Morchella Marinara
7. Morel Tempura
8. Wood Nymph Gravy
9. The Official Minnesota State Dinner
10. Charcoal—Grilled Morels Stuffed with Walleye Pike
11. Morelkies
12. Morel Dust Soup

SHORE LUNCH

Eating fresh morels fried in butter over an impromptu camp fire in the field with a group of friends is a joyful experience in contradictions. You sit there on a stump or rock, often covered with mud and wood ticks, dressed in torn clothing. Your hands and forearms are scraped and bleeding from crawling through prickly ash, more formidable than the most vicious barbed wire. Each wound evokes a memory of a morel and the subsequent scars you will wear as proud badges of determination and success. You are a rag-tag lot, appearing much more like Robin Hood's gang than the Sheriff of Nottingham and his group of dandy lackeys.

On the inside, you feel anything but poor. When you smell the morels frying in the butter, watch them sizzle and give up their juices, taste, chew and swallow the mushrooms, have a swig straight from the bottle of a $5 Beaujolais, and eat the torn chunk of chewy French bread you use to mop up the pan, you have actualized a blessing kings pray to gods for.

You are far away from the frantic, desolate pursuit of material wealth and all of its hollow rewards. You are a long way from shopping in stores and the gewgaw fare of modern consumerism. You are alive and very well.

Directions:

Carry a black cast-iron pan, a loaf of French bread, a pound of butter, and a book of matches on your hunt. Find and pick morels. Start a small fire and let it burn down to hot coals. Throw a chunk of butter in the pan. Melt the butter until it foams. Throw in the morels. Stir the mushrooms with a stick and cook until tender. Dive in. Excess butter and morel juice should be mopped up with a hunk of bread. Eat the bread.

SAUTÉED MORELS "NE PLUS ULTRA*"

1 room morels   ½ lemon
3 tablespoons unsalted butter   1 loaf French bread

This is definitely the recipe to use celebrating the first morels of spring.

Melt the butter over medium high heat in a cast iron skillet. Toss in the morels (if using dried morels, remember to rehydrate them first). Sauté the morels for four minutes and squeeze in the fresh lemon juice. Scoop onto plates or into bowls. Pour the remaining pan juices over the top of the morels. Use French bread to sop up the juices after you have hoovered down the morels. This recipe should serve four, but someone will always make sure it doesn't.

Ne plus ultra (Latin). The extreme or utmost point; hence, perfection; literally, nothing beyond.

MORCHELLA EGGSCULENTA

6 eggs
½ cup milk
1 roon morels
½ teaspoon fresh ground black pepper
½ teaspoon crushed red pepper (for color & kick)

4 tablespoons butter
1 tablespoon minced parsley
2 cloves garlic, minced
¼ cup brandy
1 pinch of salt

Melt 2 tablespoons of butter in a skillet over medium high heat. Put in garlic. Twenty seconds later, put in the chopped morels and sauté for four minutes. Add the brandy. If it flames, just let it burn. Remove contents from skillet and save in a small bowl.

Lightly beat the eggs in a small mixing bowl. Add the milk, salt and both kinds of pepper.

Melt the remaining 2 tablespoons of butter in the skillet over medium high heat and pour in the egg mixture. Stir the eggs until they begin to scramble and add the brandied morel mixture. When the eggs are done, turn out onto a platter and dust with minced parsley. Serves four.

If you have an omelet pan, make a couple of two egg omelets using a tablespoon or two of the brandied morel filling for each omelet.

A garnish can be as simple as a dusting of fresh ground pepper, a sprig of parsley, an orange or lemon wedge, some red pepper sauce, or a combination of the above.

MORELS WITH BLUEGILL, RED EAR, PUMPKIN SEED, AND CALICO BREAM

1½ pounds panfish fillets
4 tablespoons butter
1 tablespoon fresh ground pepper
½ lemon
2 cloves garlic

1 medium onion
1 cup dry white wine
½ cup cream
1 roon morels
1 tablespoon chopped parsley

Wild leeks, scallions and other fresh vegetables go well with this recipe. This dish, served with salad and some crusty bread, makes a fine spring tonic kind of meal.

This recipe goes fast, so put on your tennies and preheat your oven to 500°F or as hot as it will go. While the oven is getting hot, melt 2 tablespoons of butter, grind the pepper, and find an ovenproof dish large enough to hold the fillets in one layer. Place the fish in the dish, pour the butter over them, sprinkle the entire tablespoon of pepper on the fish, and squeeze the lemon over everything.

While the oven is still preheating, melt the other 2 tablespoons of butter in a skillet, add garlic and onion and sauté about five minutes over medium high heat. Add morels and sauté four more minutes. If the oven has preheated by this time, quickly place the pan with the fish on the bottom rack of the oven for two minutes…that's right, two minutes. Set a timer.

Return to the skillet and add the dry white wine and cream. Let this boil at high heat stirring occasionally. When the timer rings, the fish will be done and the flavor of the sauce will be in full bloom. Take the skillet off the heat and the fish out of the oven. Check the fish in the center of the dish to see if they are cooked (white). If the fish is not done, return the dish to the oven for one more minute. Remove fish from oven and arrange the buttery little fillets on plates, pour the sauce with the morels over the fish, sprinkle each serving with a little of the chopped parsley and serve.

Serves four.

MORELS WITH STEAK, BLACK AND BLUE

1 steak, New York cut, 1½ inches thick,
  about 1½ pounds (room temperature)
2 tablespoons peppercorns, crushed
1 tablespoon corn oil
3 cloves garlic
3 tablespoons butter
1 scallion

1 jigger of brandy
1 cup dry red wine
1 roon morels
1 medium tomato
1 tablespoon chopped parsley
1 loaf French bread

This is the way to eat steak. It is utterly decadent and totally befitting a gustatorial orgy. You probably will have to talk to your butcher about the steak. Tell him or her exactly what you want. The butcher will be glad to be given a chance to show off and will most likely trim your steak perfectly.

Dredge the steak in the crushed pepper completely covering the steak and pushing the pepper into the fabric of the meat with your fingers. Don't worry about the amount of pepper—use it all.

Now heat a good-sized cast-iron skillet over high heat. Add the oil. Let it get hot. Add the three cloves of garlic and swim them around for about 30 seconds (they will be brown). Skim them out and set aside.

Lay the steak in the pan and reduce the heat to medium high after one minute. There will be some smoke with this recipe, so use your range hood, disconnect your smoke alarm temporarily, and warn your neighbors not to call the fire department. Cook the steak for three more minutes on this side, then turn and cook four minutes on the second side. Stand it on edge to sear and brown the fat for two minutes and do the same with the other edge. Lay the steak back down and turn it once a minute while it cooks for another five minutes. Remove to a warm platter.

Pour off the fat and the loose peppercorns from the skillet, add one tablespoon of butter and the chopped scallion. The heat should still be set at medium high. Stir the butter around a bit to remove any bits of steak and pepper from the skillet bottom. Add the brandy and the wine, toss in the morels and let everything reduce for about four minutes. Whisk in two tablespoons of butter and stir for one minute. Pour the entire mixture over the steak, then place the skillet back on the burner, halve the tomato and place in skillet face down.

Sprinkle the steak with the chopped parsley and cut a few half-inch-thick slices from the steak. With a spatula, place the tomatoes on the platter at each end of the steak, tuck a loaf of French bread under your arm, grab the platter and start running. The steak will feed two people. The other person will find you. The bread is used to sop up the morel and steak gravy.

MORCHELLA MARINARA

2 tablespoons olive oil

2 cloves garlic, minced

1 medium onion, chopped

2 cans whole tomatoes, each 1 pound, 12 ounces,
  or 1½ quarts home-canned tomatoes,
  or an equivalent quantity of fresh tomatoes

6 canned anchovies or 1 tablespoon
  anchovy paste

1 tablespoon fresh ground black pepper

2 tablespoons fresh or 1 teaspoon dried
  sweet basil

1 teaspoon dried oregano

1 tablespoon chopped parsley

1 green pepper, chopped

1 red bell pepper, chopped

1 roon morels

Morchella Marinara is served over pasta. This recipe should serve four to six, so make your spaghetti accordingly. Marinara also freezes well in case you have a mind to making up a batch of it.

Heat the olive oil in a heavy four-quart saucepan, add the garlic and onion, and sauté over medium heat for about five minutes. Puree the tomatoes and anchovies in blender or food processor and add to the saucepan. Add pepper, basil, oregano and parsley. Stir and bring to a boil. Reduce heat and simmer, uncovered, until the sauce is quite thick. The amount of time this takes depends on the amount of liquid in the tomatoes. It will probably be close to an hour before the sauce is thick. Meanwhile...

Medium dice the pepper and coarsely chop the morels. Add these to the sauce 15 minutes before you plan to serve it. The sauce should be at a simmer at this time. If you have stopped the sauce when thick and held it for a while, that's fine. Just bring it back up to a simmer before you add the peppers and morels.

MOREL TEMPURA

1½ cups tempura batter:
  1 cup flour
  3 tablespoons cornstarch
  1 tablespoon oil
  9 tablespoons lukewarm water
½ roon morels (halved)
1 green pepper, chopped to same size as morels

1 red pepper, chopped to same size as morels
1 onion, chopped in large pieces
2 stalks celery, cut to same size as morels
1 zucchini, cut to same size as morels
½ pound shrimp, about the same size as morels,
  cleaned but with tails intact
1 bunch parsley
  Oil for deep frying

Deep-fried morels are a favorite of many despite the fact that the batter is often too heavy. Pronto pup batter is fitting for a hot dog, but I think morels would taste better dressed in a polyester leisure suit than in a thick, greasy batter. Tempura batter is light and lacy and will soon become a favorite of yours.

Mix the first three items of the batter and add the lukewarm water slowly mixing gently to form a smooth batter. Let this batter rest a few minutes while you heat the oil to 350°F and prepare the other ingredients.

When everything is prepared, gather the eaters around for some tableside cooking. To heat the oil, use a sturdy pot, wok, deep fryer, or whatever you can rig up. Make sure the pot of hot oil is steady and will not tip. When all is ready you dip the same number of an ingredient as there are anxious mouths awaiting (no more than six or you won't enjoy yourself).

Thoroughly dry the reconstituted morels, washed veggies and shrimp with paper towels. Let's start with the morels. Dip the morels into the batter using your fingers or tongs. It's good to leave a little of the tidbit exposed. Shake off excess batter gently, carefully lower it into the hot oil and deep-fry until golden brown. Serve each guest one of the morels and proceed to the next ingredient.

This is a relaxed, gentle, intimate, and delicious meal if you don't invite too many people.

An alternative presentation is to fry the food in batches keeping the cooked pieces on a cookie sheet on paper towels in a 250°F oven. When all food is fried, serve the entire platter and stand back.

An excellent dipping sauce can be made by mixing ½ cup vinegar, ½ cup soy sauce, 1 teaspoon chili oil and ½ cup minced scallions. This sauce can be put in one central bowl or in small individual bowls. Individual bowls are suggested. People get downright nasty when it comes to dipping and it is not beyond the realm of possibility to end up with teeth marks on unwary fingers. The recipe should be doubled if there are double-dippers in the group.

WOOD NYMPH GRAVY

¼ cup butter

2 cloves garlic, minced

½ onion, chopped

1 roon morels

¼ cup flour

2 cups morel liquor

½ lemon

½ cup dry white wine

¼ teaspoon fresh nutmeg, grated

This treatment of the morel is a classic European traditional approach.

Melt butter in medium saucepan over medium heat. Add garlic, onion and morels and sauté for about five minutes. Mix in flour and cook for another three to four minutes. Now, slowly add morel liquor while stirring with a whisk. The mixture will stay partially thick during this process. Squeeze in the lemon juice and whisk. Pour in the wine and whisk. Put in the nutmeg and whisk until the gravy becomes medium thick. Remove from heat and ladle it over toast, rice, noodles, biscuits, pheasant, duck, beef, lamb, bullfrog, elk, potatoes and carp.

Serves four.

Toast is considered the carrier for the gravy, but as suggested, Wood Nymph Gravy goes well with other offerings. A variation of this recipe calls for the substitution of ½ cup cream for the wine. Many morel purists prefer their morels served this way. Try both ways if you have the morels and make up your own mind. You may have to try each of them three or four times before you make up your mind.

THE OFFICIAL MINNESOTA STATE DINNER

4 ounces wild rice
4 cups lightly salted water
3 tablespoons butter
1 medium onion, chopped
1 roon morels
1 cup flour

1 cup cornmeal
4 tablespoons corn oil (or more as needed)
4 walleye fillets
1 lemon, cut into wedges
1 tablespoon parsley, minced
salt and pepper

This recipe is some of the best eating that the outdoors has to offer. Anytime that walleye, wild rice and morels can be obtained, you and your friends are in for a treat worth fighting for.

Wash the wild rice thoroughly and place in a heavy saucepan with 4 cups lightly salted water. Bring to a boil, reduce heat and simmer, covered, for 45 minutes. Uncover, fluff with fork, simmer another five minutes, and drain.

In two tablespoons of butter sauté the onion over medium high heat just until the onion turns clear, about four to five minutes. Add the morels and sauté for four minutes, add the cooked wild rice and mix. Keep warm in 200°F oven.

Mix flour and cornmeal together in a bowl and season to taste with salt and pepper. In a cast-iron skillet, heat 2 tablespoons of oil over medium high heat. Dredge the walleye fillets in the flour/cornmeal mixture, and put them, two at a time, into the skillet. Reduce to medium heat. When brown on one side, turn. Test the thick part of the fillet with a fork; when it turns from translucent to pure white it is done. Cook no longer. Place on a warm platter and put in the warm oven with the rice.

Follow the same instructions with the other two fillets. When finished sautéing the fish, it is time to assemble the plates. It is nice to have four dinner plates warming in the oven. By this time your oven is getting crowded. On each plate, place a golden brown walleye fillet and a couple of lemon wedges. Alongside the walleye, place a generous helping of the wild rice and morel mixture.

Additional garnishes are up to you, but a favorite of mine is to use the remaining tablespoon of butter in the heated skillet in which the walleye was fried. Swirl the butter around until it foams over high heat, squeeze in a little lemon juice and then fling in a tablespoon of finely minced parsley. Swirl this mixture around in the pan for a few seconds and pour a little of it over each fillet.

CHARCOAL-GRILLED MORELS STUFFED WITH WALLEYE PIKE

I believe this is the best recipe Jerry Petermeier has ever created. The flavor is so distinguished and mouth-watering that each time I have prepared it, people have actually burst out laughing in response to its sheer deliciousness.

The last time I cooked this meal, my morel-hawking brother-in-law, Kiki, had brought over a hundred extra-large whole fresh morels he had found the day before. We prepared the recipe and stood there watching the morels cook, basting them with butter and sniffing the aroma. Kiki snapped open a can of cold beer and had a sip. One of the smaller morels was cooked in advance of the other larger ones, and he thought it only admirable to test the dish before we served the entire batch to the rest of the family. He picked up the cooked stuffed morel with his fingers and ate the whole thing in a couple of bites. He laughed out loud, wiped the butter off of his chin with the back of his hand, and had another sip of beer. He leaned back against the big old maple tree, folded his arms across his chest and said quietly, "I wonder what the poor Republicans are doing today?"

Directions:

Make the stuffing by steaming or poaching fresh walleye fillets; flake the fish in a bowl with a fork and drizzle with melted butter. Stuff as many of your whole fresh morels as you choose. Skewer the stuffed morels, baste them with butter and place them over a low charcoal fire (not too hot). Turn the kabobs periodically, continuing to baste with butter until the mushrooms are cooked. Slow cooking works best. A slice of pepperoni between the mushrooms adds a zip of flavor and a pleasing splash of color.

MORELKIES

½ cup water chestnuts

6 slices bacon, blanched two minutes
   in boiling water, drained and cut in half

12 good-sized fresh or reconstituted dried
   morel halves

4 bamboo skewers soaked in water
   for ten minutes

½ cup melted butter and basting brush

These tasty tidbits can be assembled and served quickly and easily. My friend John refers to these morel halves as "pelts." I'm not sure, but I think he is planning to make a hat out of a bunch of the larger pelts. I warned him about going into the woods wearing such a hat during morel season. Odds are great that someone will try to rip his head off.

To assemble the "morelkie," take a chestnut and wrap it with half a bacon slice. Then, wrap a morel pelt at a 90° angle to the bacon and skewer the whole thing onto the bamboo skewer. Add two more of these setups to complete one skewer.

Cook the morelkies on a hibachi or charcoal grill five or six inches above the coals, or in a 400°F oven on a cookie sheet. Brush each morelkie with butter two times while cooking. The total cooking time in either case is about six to nine minutes.

Serves four as an appetizer.

MOREL DUST SOUP

½ cup morel dust
¼ cup butter
¼ cup flour
2½ cups morel liquor

1 cup cream
½ cup dry sherry
¼ teaspoon fresh grated nutmeg
1 tablespoon chopped parsley

Get out those dried stems and broken pieces of morels that you have been hoarding and one jar of morel liquor. Throw a cupful of these morels into a food processor or blender and pulverize them to make the morel dust.

Melt the butter over medium heat in a medium saucepan. When the butter is melted, mix in flour, stirring it around for about two minutes. Next, slowly add the morel liquor, whisking it in the pan for about one minute. Add the morel dust and continue to whisk. Add the cream and keep on whisking. Add the sherry and keep on whisking. Add the nutmeg and keep on whisking. When all this is hot enough, but not boiling (about two to three minutes), pour into bowls, dust with parsley and serve.

Makes four servings.

INTERNATIONALLY SOUGHT; LAUNCHING SPORES, MOREL SEX WITH INTENT TO PROPAGATE AND CAUSING FOREST FIRES & EXTREME BEHAVIOR

WANTED BY FBI*

*FUNGAL BUREAU OF INVESTIGATION

MOREL MUSHROOM

10M
Entered
I.O. 5326
5-16-85

FBI No. 222 M

18　M　R　00N　8

ALIASES: Morel, Morchella deliosa, Big Foot, Paul's Bunyan, Moby Morel, Cone Head, Whiteridge, Bob.

IDM 13182213-47-9-10-83

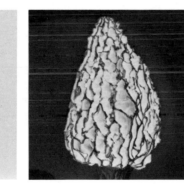

Photographs taken 1985

DESCRIPTION
DATE OF BIRTH: Every Spring
PLACE OF BIRTH: Widespread
HEIGHT: 1/4" to 14"
WEIGHT: Varies
BUILD: Hollow throughout pits and ridges
HAIR: None

CRIMINAL RECORD
Morels have defied cultivation for years

CAUTION
MORELS ARE ELUSIVE AND EXPERTS AT THE ART OF CAMOUFLAGE

IF YOU HAVE INFORMATION CONCERNING THIS MUSHROOM PLEASE CONTACT YOUR LOCAL ROON PLATOON

James Lang

Director
Fungal Bureau of Investigation
Long Lake, Minnesota

Identification Order 72255
March 6, 1989

THEY DON'T PICK UM LIKE THEY USED TO

By Lee M. Muggli

Spring had once again come to Minnesota, bringing warm gentle rains and those wonderful earthy odors from the deep woods. It was a time of restlessness and agitation for a young boy. I had been confined in school for what seemed an eternity and anxiously awaited summer when I would be free once again to roam the fields and forests. Already the landscape was greening. As I sat in class, my mind was not on my schoolwork but on morels, or merkles as the old folks called them.

Grandpa had promised to take me merkling on Saturday. The time was right. Already the oak leaves were the size of squirrel's ears and the lilacs were beginning to show some color. Grandpa had told me that the trillium was just starting to bloom in the woods and that he had found a handful of merkles on the south slope. "It won't be long now, lad," he said. "Come Saturday they should be poppin' in the woods." Grandpa knew. Grandpa always knew and he was always ready.

Friday night after supper Grandpa motioned me to follow him into the pantry. It was a place filled with magical odors of herbs and spices and dozens of jars and tins from an entire year of collecting and preserving. There were bottles of pure maple syrup Grandpa had laboriously put up in March during sugar time. But what he was looking for was hidden away on the shelves in the very back corner. He took one jar from the shelf and slid off the wire retainer that held down the glass lid. "Merkles!" he whispered, and gave me a wink. "Open it," I said impatiently. Grandpa took his time. He did most things slowly these days. He seemed never to be

in a hurry but was never late for anything either.

Off came the lid and the small crowded pantry was suddenly filled with a new odor that overwhelmed all the dried herbs and spices. It was a wonderful smell. I stuck my nose into the jar mouth and sniffed. "Easy now, lad," said Grandpa. "We'll fry up a little batch later." We did so, filling the house with that wonderful smell that would linger through the night.

When they were fried Grandpa hesitated before handing me a fork. "Now get a good look at them merkles before you gobble them all up. You'll need to remember what they look like when we go out in the mornin'." They had swelled up in the hot water before being put in a pan with a little butter, and they looked just like I remembered them from last year. I slept restlessly that night dreaming of merkles half hidden among the bedstraw and prickly ash. Even at breakfast the next morning I imagined seeing them in my oatmeal. I was ready.

Almost before I realized it, I was heading into the woods carrying two wicker baskets. In my excitement I ran ahead of Grandpa. I slowed down and dropped back when I heard Grandpa say sharply, "Slow down and be quiet before you spook um all." Grandpa, who walked with two canes these days, was taking his time and being careful where he stepped. He would look from side to side and occasionally behind him as we walked along.

We hadn't gone far into the woods when Grandpa said, "Stop! You're going to stomp um all to pieces." I stopped and slowly looked around. I thought to myself, stomp what all to pieces?

Slowly Grandpa raised the cane in his right hand and pointed. "There's three right over there", he said. I quickly bent down, cut them off, brushed them clean and dropped them in a basket. As I did so, Grandpa pointed with the cane in his left hand and said, "There's a bunch over there and a couple over here…"

Things soon got really busy then. I had a hard time keeping up with Grandpa's pointing. I even managed to spot a few merkles on my own.

We moved on. A minute later Grandpa started pointing again. "Over here. Over there. Some more behind you", he said. Grandpa sounded excited. How could that be? Grandpa never got excited.

And then it happened. I guess it was bound to happen. I heard a muffled thud behind me and turned to see Grandpa sprawled face down on the ground with his canes sticking out to the sides. In his excitement he had raised both canes at the same time to point at all the merkles and had lost his balance.

He got to his feet with the aid of a small tree near him. "You look like you need a rest", he said. "Let's sit over there on that log awhile. No sense in rushing when we've got all day." "OK", I said, "I've already got this first basket about full and it's getting heavy."

We sat on the log and Grandpa got his pipe going. After a while I asked, "Grandpa, have folks always picked merkles?" Grandpa didn't answer right away but seemed to be trying to remember something. When it looked as if he had his thoughts together he replied, "When I was a youngster about your age I remember hearing about how the Indians went about getting their merkles. The tribe would send out scouts to spot a sizable herd of merkles. When one was located they would make preparations for the following day. They checked out the surrounding terrain and hoped the wind would be right. Just before dawn they moved out to circle the herd making sure they moved in first from downwind."

I had a feeling I had heard Grandpa tell a similar story before. Some details seemed vaguely familiar. I wanted to ask, but Grandpa didn't like to be interrupted when he was telling one of his stories. Grandpa drew in on his pipe and let out the smoke slowly before he continued.

"When all the Indians were in place they began to yell and wave their arms. The merkles would jump up, mill around a bit, and then take off. The Indians drove them toward a cliff, and in their panic, the merkles went right over the edge. The whole herd would end up in a pile at the bottom."

Was that all there was to it? I wondered. Another puff on the pipe and I found out.

"Now that the fun was over it was time for the work to begin. All the Indians including the women and children helped with the harvest. The merkles had to be butchered. Most were cut up into strips and dried in the sun on racks that the Indians built right there on the spot. Many merkle hides got tanned. Later some would be made into storage bags and others into new winter moccasins. They had a good non-skid surface that was ideal for walking over snow and ice. The Indians didn't waste a single merkle. The work often lasted for three or four days, and in the

Illustration by Tom Paul Larson

evenings there were great feasts of fresh merkles. In areas where there were no handy cliffs, the Indians would run the merkles into a box canyon. Either way they usually got enough merkles to last the whole year."

Now I was sure Grandpa had told this story before, but I thought it had something to do with buffalo or wild horses. I wanted to say so to Grandpa but thought better of it. Grandpa's memory might not be what it used to be, but there was nothing wrong with his eyes when it came to spotting merkles.

"Leave that full basket here," said Grandpa. "We'll pick it up on the way back. After we fill that second basket we'll head for home."

"I hope we don't miss a single one," I said.

"We don't need to get every one," said Grandpa. "It looks like a good season and we should get all we need. It's always good to leave a few for seed."

The last thing I heard before I went to bed that night was a gentle but firm reminder from Grandpa. "When your friends ask you where we got um, mum's the word."

PHOTO CREDITS

Dried morels are available directly from:

Incredible Wild Edibles, Inc., William Jaspers, III, Pres., Dept. RN, P.O. Box 23544, Minneapolis, MN 55423, (612) 861-1248